MEGA BOOKS

DINOSAURS

NINA FILIPEK
AND SOPHIE GILES

Gareth Stevens
PUBLISHING

BE A SUPER SPOTTER

Study these pictures and look out for them as you read this book. Can you answer the super spotter questions?

Who do these sharp teeth belong to?

Who uses these bony bumps for protection?

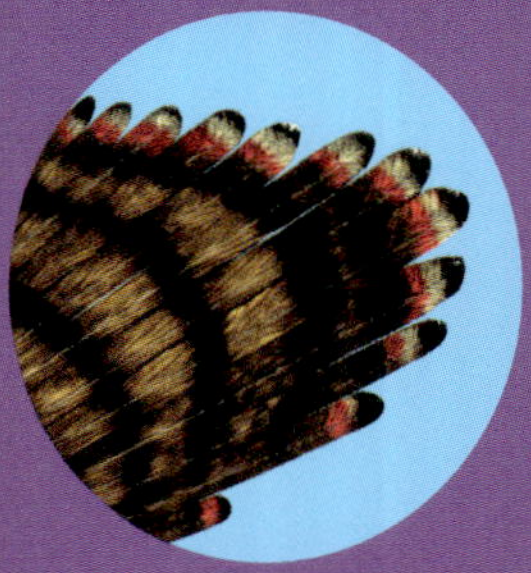

Whose feathers are these?

Whose fossil is this?

Please visit our website, www.garethstevens.com. For a free color catalog of all our high-quality books, call toll free 1-800-542-2595 or fax 1-877-542-2596.

Published in 2025 by
Gareth Stevens Publishing
2544 Clinton St.
Buffalo, NY 14224

Written by: Nina Filipek and Sophie Giles

Images: (all Shutterstock unless noted) front cover: DM7, Photobank gallery; back cover: DM7, Jean-Michel Girard; p1: Leonello Calvetti; p3: Catmando, Twin Design, Michael Rosskothen, Elenarts, Vector Goddess, Elenarts, m.pilot, DM7, Leonello Calvetti, Valentyna Chukhlyebova, Michael Rosskothen, miha de; pp4–5: Michael Rosskothen, Linda Bucklin, Catmando, somyot pattana, Matt Antonino, Christian Delbert; pp6–7: Leonello Calvetti, Catmando, David Herraez Calzada, Twin Design, Marcio Jose Bastos Silva; pp8–9: Michael Rosskothen, Leonello Calvetti, dimair, Mikkel Bigandt; pp10–11: Elenarts, Linda Bucklin, Axente Vlad, Vector Goddess, Leonello Calvetti, m.pilot; pp12–13: Elena Schweitzer, DM7/Adobe Stock, Baciu; pp14–15: Michael Rosskothen, Linda Bucklin, Leonello Calvetti, Africa Studio, zcw, STILLFX; pp16–17: DM7, Michael Rosskothen, Leonello Calvetti; pp18–19: Michael Rosskothen, Leonello Calvetti, Catmando; pp20–21: Leonello Calvetti, Catmando, Michael Rosskothen; pp22–23: Jean-Michel Girard, Michael Rosskothen, Catmando; pp24–25: Elenarts, Michael Rosskothen, Leonello Calvetti; pp26–27: Lukasz Kurbiel, Valentyna Chukhlyebova, Michael Rosskothen, Leonello Calvetti; pp28–29: Michael Rosskothen, Catmando, Sombra; pp30–31: PandaWild, Elenarts, DM7, Catmando, miha de.

Cataloging-in-Publication Data

Names: Filipek, Nina. | Giles, Sophie.
Title: Dinosaurs / by Nina Filipek and Sophie Giles.
Description: Buffalo, NY : Gareth Stevens Publishing, 2025. | Series: Mega books
Identifiers: ISBN 9781482467963 (pbk.) | ISBN 9781482467970 (library bound) | ISBN 9781482467987 (ebook)
Subjects: LCSH: Dinosaurs--Juvenile literature.
Classification: LCC QE861.5 F47 2025 | DDC 567.9--dc23

Printed in the United States of America

CPSIA compliance information: Batch #CSGS25: For further information contact Gareth Stevens at 1-800-542-2595.

CONTENTS

TERRIBLE REPTILES

Dinosaurs lived over 66 million years ago at a time when Earth was covered in forests, deserts, and shallow seas. Some dinosaurs were much larger than animals that are alive today. For example, *Diplodocus* was almost as tall as two giraffes standing on top of each other!

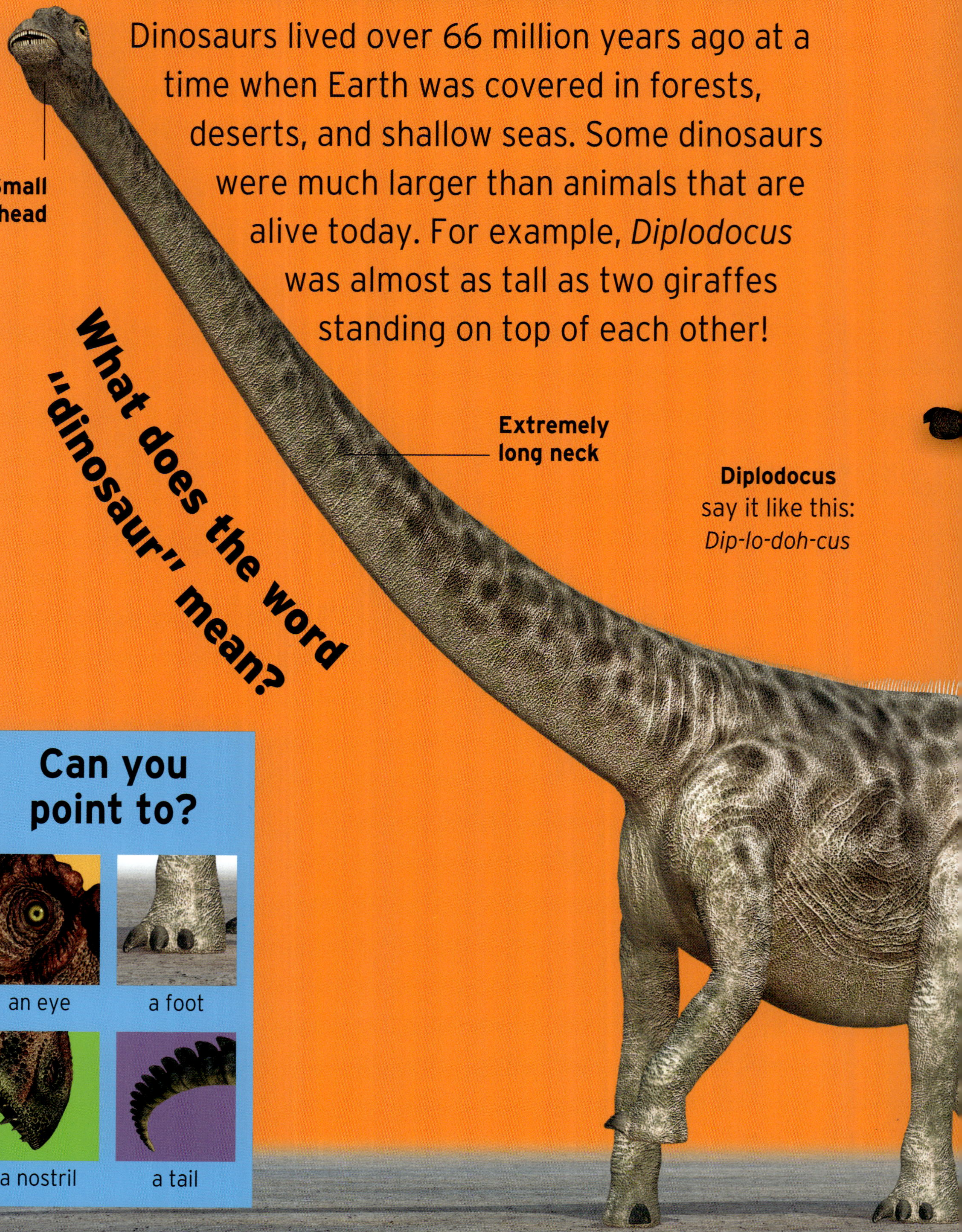

Diplodocus
say it like this:
Dip-lo-doh-cus

What does the word "dinosaur" mean?

Can you point to?

an eye

a foot

a nostril

a tail

Giganotosaurus
Ji-gan-oh-toe-saw-ruhs

Prehistoric animals

Other animals lived on Earth at the same time as the dinosaurs. These included insects, such as giant dragonflies, prehistoric fish, and crocodiles, such as *Kaprosuchus*.

Compsognathus
Comp-sog-nay-thus

Different sizes

Not all dinosaurs were big. Look how small *Compsognathus* was compared to *Giganotosaurus*!

Kaprosuchus
Kap-row-sue-cus

Long tail for balance

Dinosaur names

The word "dinosaur" means "terrible reptile." Dinosaur names can be difficult to spell because scientists name them using Greek or Latin words.

FOSSIL FINDS

We know dinosaurs existed because their fossils have been found in many places around the world. A fossil is a bone, tooth, or footprint that was buried in a layer of soft mud and, over millions of years, turned into stone.

Muscle modeling

When different bones from the same dinosaur are found, scientists can start to put them together to recreate its skeleton. Computer programs are used to add muscles and skin to the skeleton so we can see what the animal may have looked like.

Allosaurus
Al-oh-saw-ruhs

This is what we think *Allosaurus* may have looked like, but we have no way of knowing what color it really was!

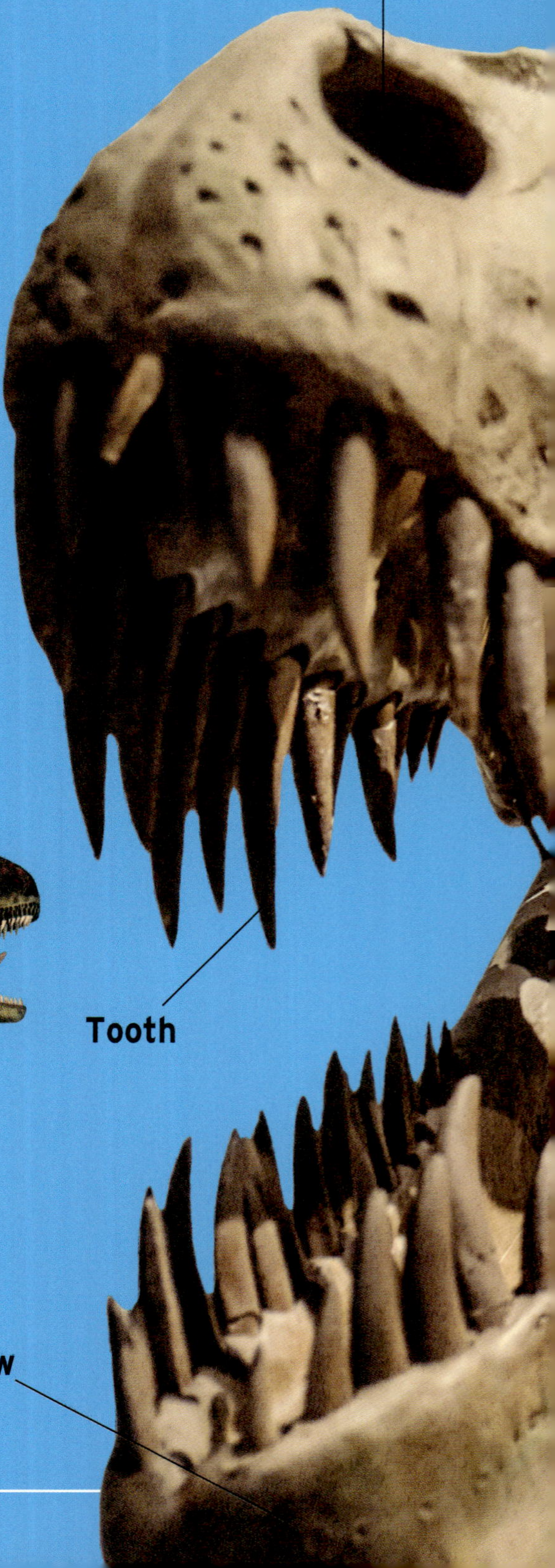

Nest egg

Most dinosaurs hatched from an egg. Fossil eggs have been found with baby dinosaurs inside them. Some dinosaurs laid as many as 20 eggs at a time.

Footprints

Sometimes we find dinosaur footprints. Millions of years ago, a dinosaur walked in some soft, sticky mud and left this footprint behind. We can see that it had three toes.

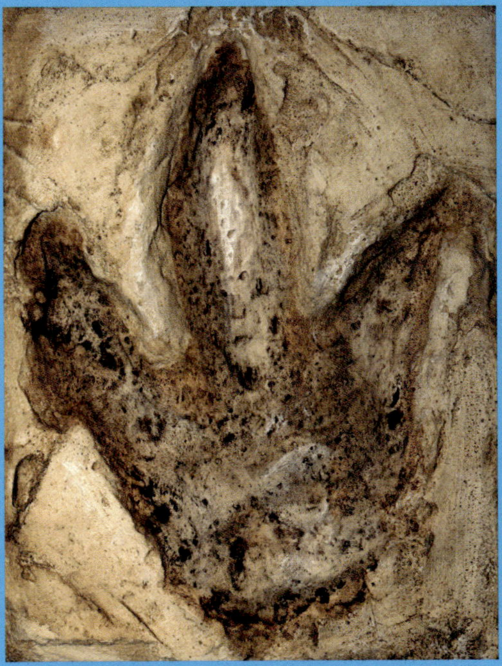

How are fossils made?

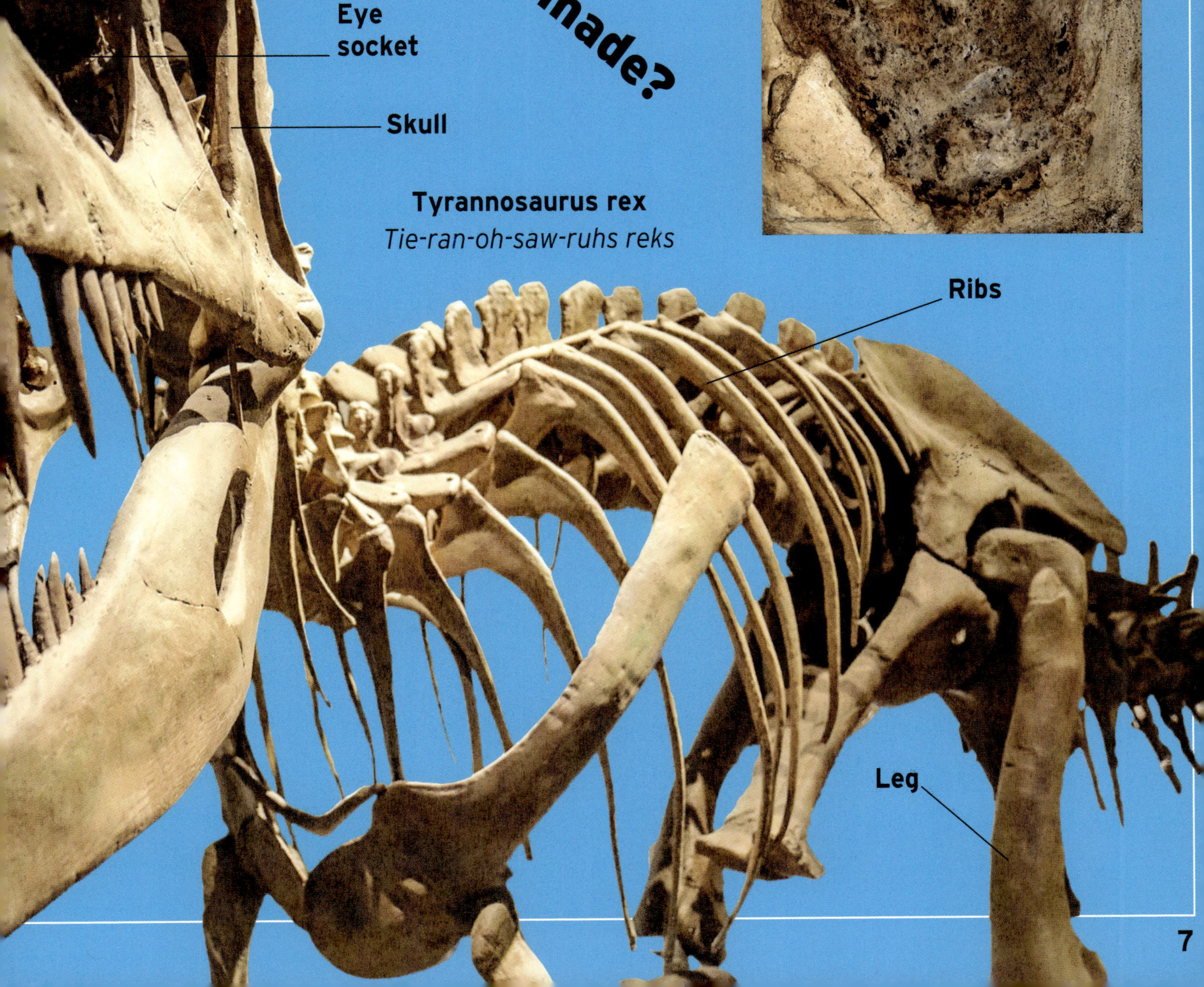

Tyrannosaurus rex
Tie-ran-oh-saw-ruhs reks

FIRST AND BIGGEST

The first dinosaur skeleton to be discovered and named was *Megalosaurus*, meaning "great lizard." Its bones were found in England in 1824. Since then, fossils from over 700 different kinds of dinosaurs have been found.

How do we know that Megalosaurus existed?

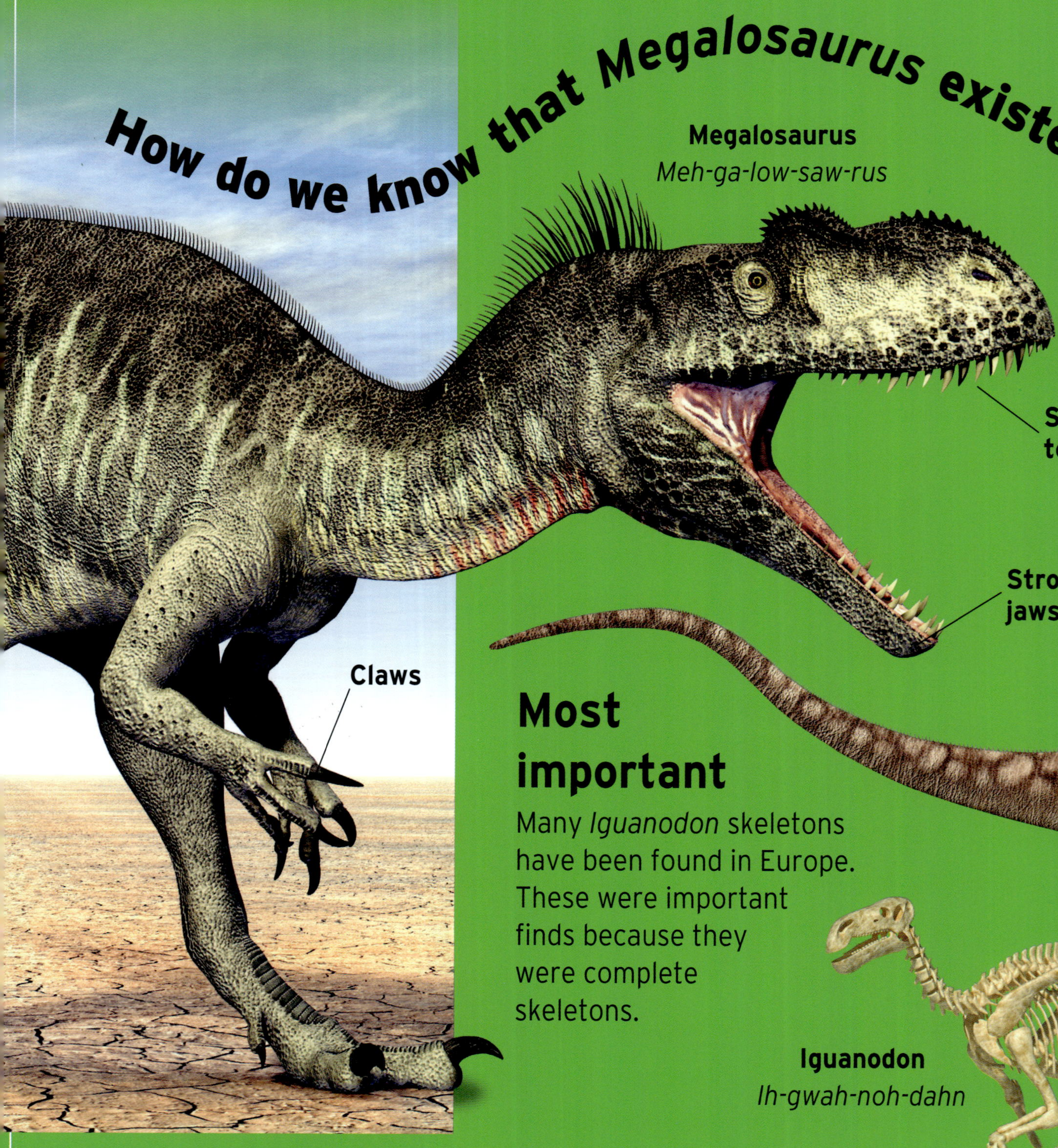

Most important

Many *Iguanodon* skeletons have been found in Europe. These were important finds because they were complete skeletons.

Triceratops
Try-ser-uh-tops

Neck and neck

Bones from one of the world's biggest dinosaurs, *Dreadnoughtus*, were first discovered in Argentina in 2014. It was as tall as a seven-story building and the length of two buses! Its neck was almost as long as its body and tail put together.

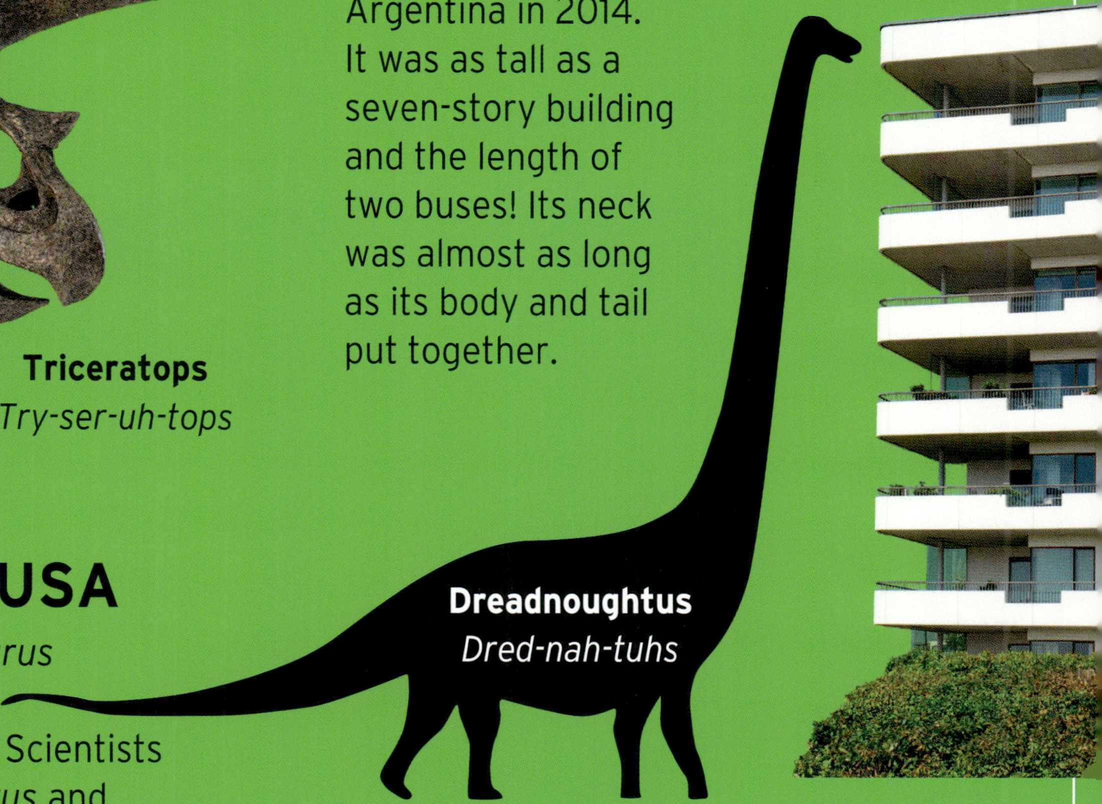

Dreadnoughtus
Dred-nah-tuhs

First in the USA

The first *Tyrannosaurus* skeleton was found in the United States. Scientists know that *Stegosaurus* and *Triceratops* lived there too because they have found their skeletons.

Argentinosaurus
Ar-jehn-ti-noh-saw-ruhs

How big?

Only a few *Argentinosaurus* leg and backbones have been found, but scientists have used them to estimate that it was between 72 and 130 feet (22 and 40 m) long.

WHAT WE KNOW

We know that some of the biggest dinosaurs had the smallest brains and were not very bright. Smaller dinosaurs, such as *Compsognathus*, had large brains for their size. They would have been clever and cunning.

Which dinosaur was clever?

Argentinosaurus
Ar-jehn-ti-noh-saw-ruhs

- Weighed as much as 12 adult African elephants!
- 72-130 feet (22-40 m) long
- It had a small brain for a large dinosaur.

Turkey

Compsognathus
Comp-sog-nay-thus

- Same size as a turkey
- 3.2 feet (1 m) long
- It had a large brain for a small dinosaur.

What color were they?

Scientists don't know what color many of the dinosaurs were, but some of them may have been brightly colored to attract a mate, or the same color as their surroundings to help them hide from other dinosaurs.

Maiasaura
May-ah-saw-ruh

What did dinosaurs eat?

The shape of a dinosaur's teeth can tell us what it was likely to eat. For example, some plant eaters had flat teeth that were good for chewing, and meat eaters had sharp teeth that were best for tearing flesh.

Spinosaurus
Spi-noh-saw-ruhs

Dinosaur droppings!

Scientists can find out more about a dinosaur's diet by studying fossilized dinosaur poop, called coprolites!

MEAT EATERS

Meat-eating dinosaurs, or carnivores, had to be fast and fierce to catch a meal. They had powerful leg muscles for running, sharply pointed teeth for biting and long claws for grabbing hold of prey.

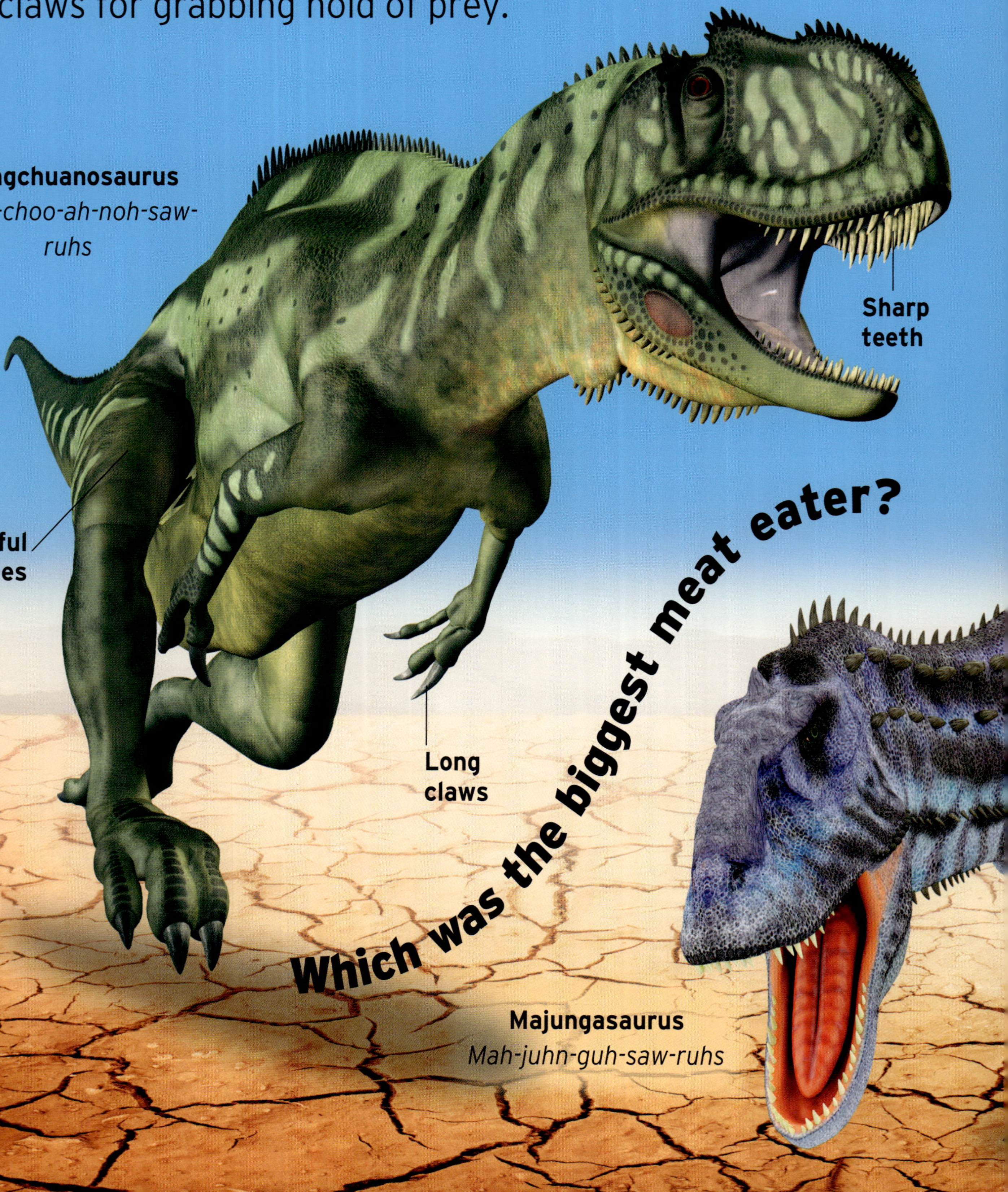

Insectivores

Some dinosaurs were insectivores. They ate insects, such as giant dragonflies and moths.

Insect trapped in fossilized tree sap, or amber

Giganotosaurus
Ji-gan-oh-toh-saw-ruhs

Big eater

Scientists are not certain of its size, but they think *Giganotosaurus* may be the largest meat eater that ever lived! Before *Gigantosaurus* was discovered in Argentina in 1993, *Tyrannosaurus rex* was thought to have been the largest carnivore.

Meaty feast

What kind of meat did dinosaurs eat? Dinosaur meat! If they got the chance, they may also have eaten alligators, small mammals, and fish. Teeth marks on fossil bones show that *Majungasaurus* even ate others of its kind!

PLANT EATERS

Plant-eating dinosaurs, or herbivores, were often much bigger than meat eaters. The biggest could not chew their food, so they swallowed stones to grind food into smaller pieces to make it easier to digest. Their huge size made it harder for carnivores to attack them.

What did herbivores eat?

Can you point to?

an eye

a beak

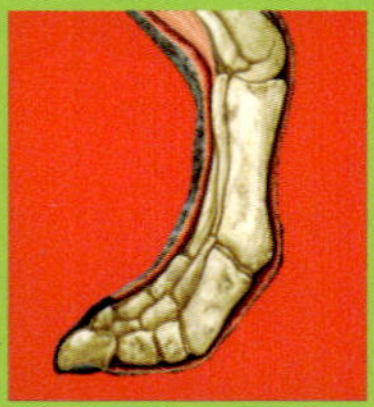

bones

Europasaurus
Yoo-roh-pah-saw-ruhs

Bony beak

Some dinosaurs had bony beaks that they used to break down tough plants and crush plant seeds.

Psittacosaurus
Sih-tah-coh-saw-ruhs

Look inside

Take a look at the insides of *Iguanodon*. The plants that it ate were broken down by the stomach and intestines.

Iguanodon
Ih-gwah-noh-dahn

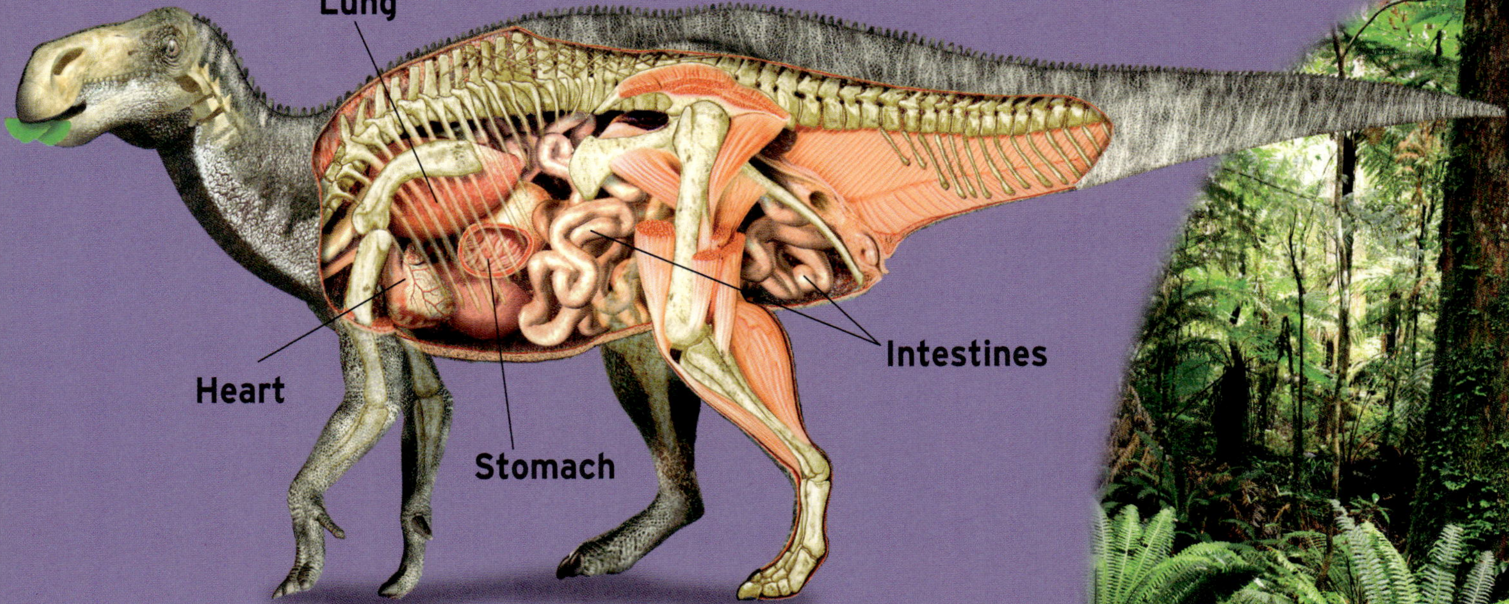

Iguanodon may have eaten ferns and ginkgos, a simple type of plant.

Ginkgo

Fern

DEADLY DINOSAURS

Tyrannosaurus rex was a dinosaur with a massive bite! It had 60 sharp teeth set in its powerful jaws. It was longer than a big bus. With a good sense of smell, it could track down its prey from far away.

Tyrannosaurus rex
Tie-ran-oh-saw-ruhs reks

Can you see its small arms?

Can you point to?

an eye

claws

teeth

Deinonychus
Die-noh-ni-cus

No biting!

Triceratops used its sharp horns to fight with others of its kind and to defend itself from *Tyrannosaurus*. Its bony neck frill was used for protection. We know this because bite and horn marks have been found on its bones!

Triceratops
Try-ser-uh-tahps

Claws and feathers

Scientists think *Deinonychus* had feathers, though it could not fly! Although its name means "terrible claw," its fearsome-looking talons were better for climbing than attacking!

Spinosaurus
Spi-noh-saw-ruhs

Thorny lizard

Spinosaurus had a row of sharp spikes along its back for protection, and its long, curved claws were perfect for attack.

BODY ARMOR

Plant-eating dinosaurs had to defend themselves from other dinosaurs who wanted to eat them. Some did this by using their body armor. *Stegosaurus* used the sharp spikes on its tail to fight off attackers.

Why did some dinosaurs have armor?

Can you point to?

a bony plate

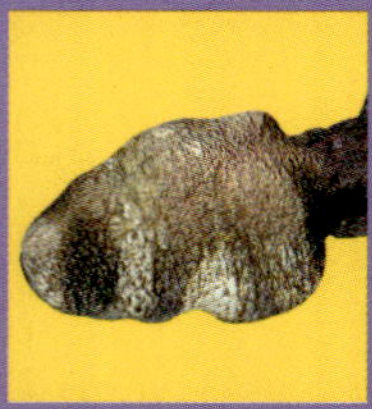
a tail club

a horn

Tail club

Ankylosaurus would swing its tail as a warning to other dinosaurs. It had a heavy club at the end! The bony bumps on its body were for protection too.

Ankylosaurus
An-key-loh-saw-ruhs

Spiky frill

Styracosaurus was a plant eater, but it looked fierce with its huge horn and spiky neck frill. It would have used this armor when attacked by other dinosaurs.

Styracosaurus
Sty-rah-cuh-saw-ruhs

SKULLS AND SPIKES

Bone-headed dinosaurs lived in North America. They had big bony bumps on their heads that they used for ramming into the bodies of rival dinosaurs. Scientists don't think they clashed heads. That would have been far too painful!

Pachycephalosaurus
Pa-kee-seff-uh-loh-saw-ruhs

Can you point to?

a mouth

a spike

an eye

How did this dinosaur use its head?

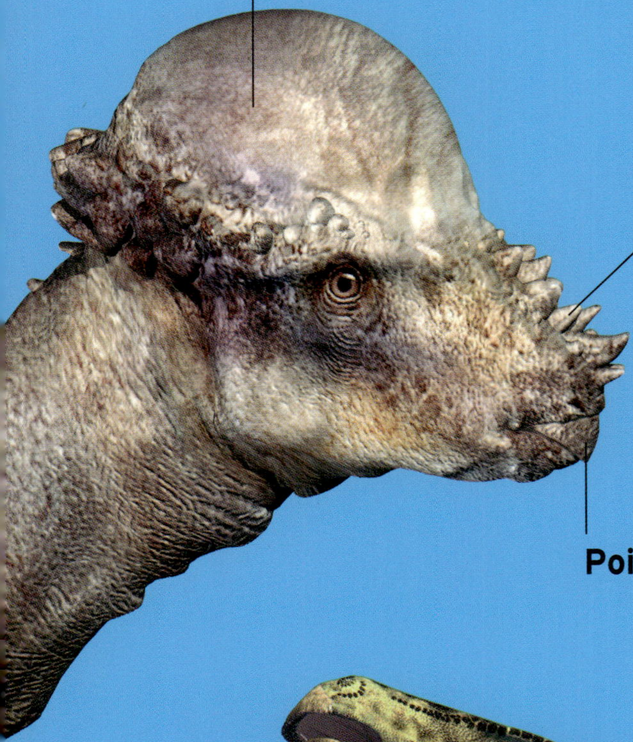

Spikey!

Kentrosaurus had two rows of plates and very long, sharp spikes along its back and down to its tail. The spikes made this small plant eater look larger and more formidable.

Kentrosaurus
Ken-troh-saw-ruhs

Gigantspinosaurus
Ji-gant-spi-noh-saw-ruhs

Don't get too close!

Gigantspinosaurus had bony plates along the top of its body and one huge, curved spike on each shoulder. This warned other dinosaurs to stay away!

CRESTS AND BILLS

The long crest on the head of this duck-billed dinosaur had a hollow tube inside that was connected to its nose. By breathing air through the tube, this dinosaur could make a low sound to warn others of danger.

Can you point to?

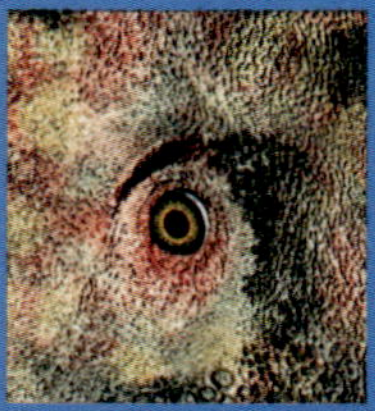
an eye

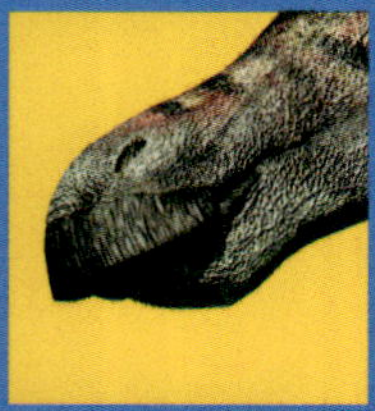
a mouth

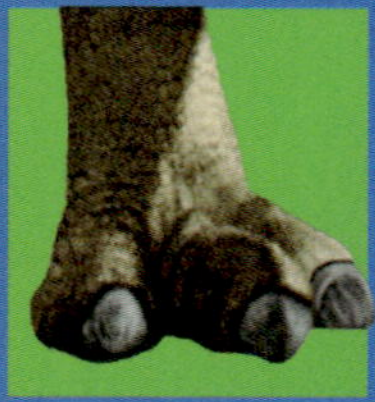
a foot

a tail

Corythosaurus
Cor-ih-thuh-saw-ruhs

Dinner plates

Corythosaurus had a flat, round crest that looked like a dinner plate. This might have been used like an amplifier to make its call louder, or to help other dinosaurs recognize it.

Dilophosaurus
Di-low-fuh-saw-ruhs

Bony ridges

Dilophosaurus had two bony crests along the top of its head. These may have helped it to attract a mate.

FEATHERED DINOSAURS

Some dinosaurs had feathers. This fast, feathered, and toothless dinosaur was *Gigantoraptor*. Despite being almost the same height and weight as a giraffe, it could run quickly on its long legs, and its large claws made it a good hunter.

Do you think this dinosaur could fly?

Enormous eggs

Gigantoraptor stood 13 feet (4 m) tall. Its eggs were giant too! At 17 inches (45 cm) long, they are among the largest dinosaur eggs ever discovered.

Feathery glider

This small reptile lived off the ground, in trees, for safety. With feathers on its arms and legs, it could glide from tree to tree.

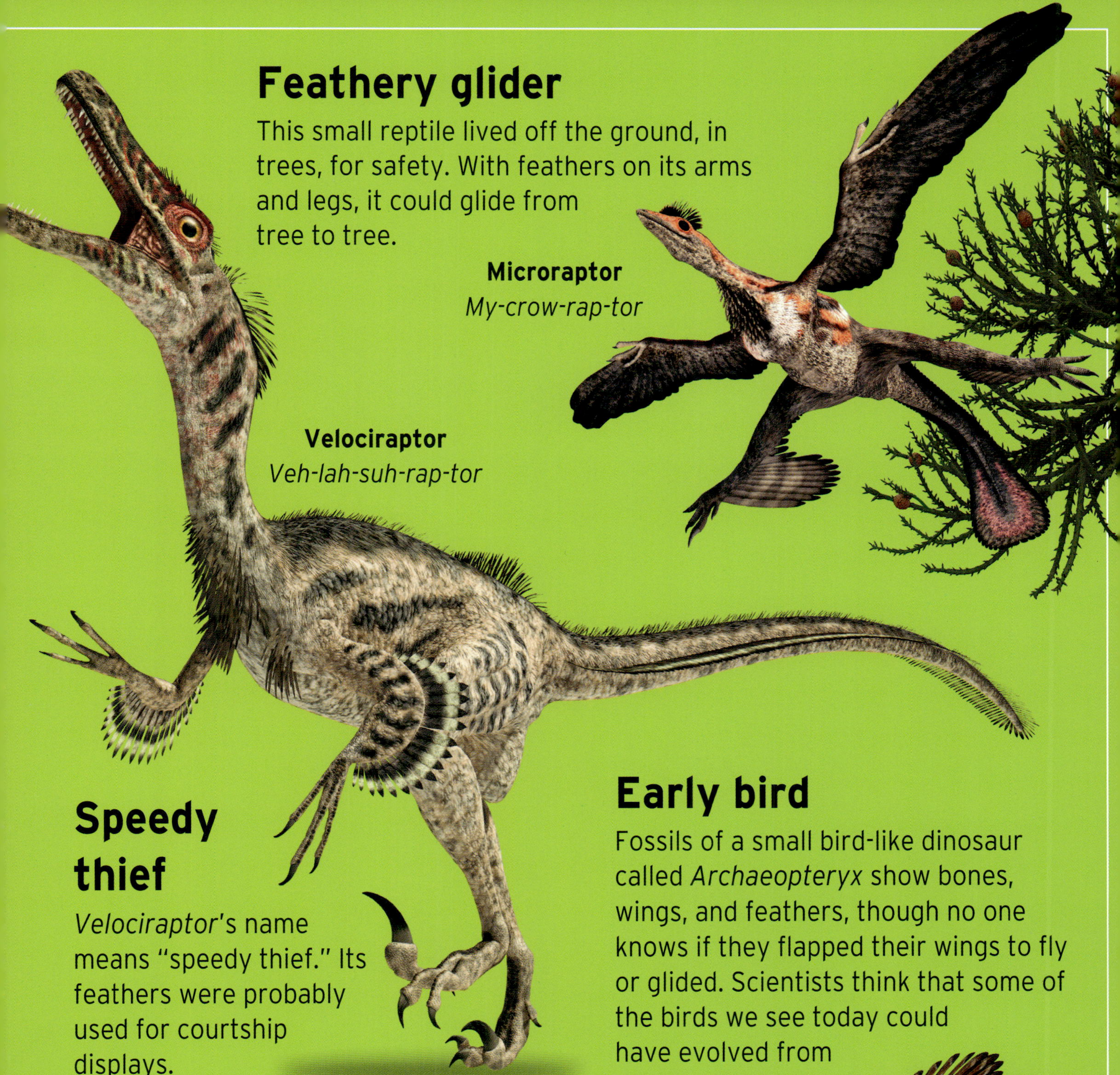

Microraptor
My-crow-rap-tor

Velociraptor
Veh-lah-suh-rap-tor

Speedy thief

Velociraptor's name means "speedy thief." Its feathers were probably used for courtship displays.

Early bird

Fossils of a small bird-like dinosaur called *Archaeopteryx* show bones, wings, and feathers, though no one knows if they flapped their wings to fly or glided. Scientists think that some of the birds we see today could have evolved from *Archaeopteryx*.

Archaeopteryx
Ar-kee-ohp-ter-iks

FLYING REPTILES

While dinosaurs ruled the land, flying reptiles called pterosaurs took to the skies. These reptiles were not dinosaurs, but they were close relations. They had long wings formed from skin and muscle stretched over thin finger bones.

Rhamphorhynchus
Ram-foh-rihn-cus

Wing finger

Like all pterosaurs, *Rhamphorhynchus* had large wings for soaring through the air. Can you spot its needlelike teeth and the diamond-shaped vane on its tail?

Fish eater

Eudimorphodon's jaws were packed with 110 sharp teeth, including six sets of fangs. The shape of its teeth suggest that it would have eaten fish, which it would swoop down to snatch from near the surface of lakes and seas.

Can you point to?

a foot

a wing tip

an eye

SEA REPTILES

Scientists have found fossils of prehistoric sea creatures too. Some had long necks and sharp teeth set in narrow, pointed jaws. These sea reptiles used their flippers like paddles to move quickly through the water.

Why did they have fins?

Can you point to?

teeth

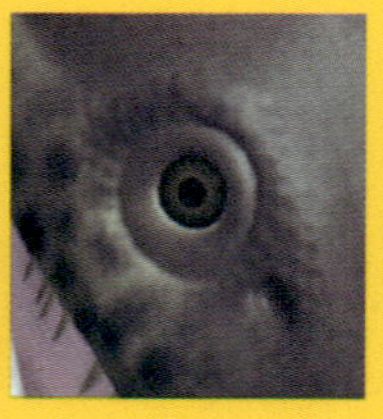
an eye

a tail

Liopleurodon

Liopleurodon was a giant of the sea. Its sharp, backward-curving teeth helped it to hold on to its prey.

Liopleurodon
Li-uh-plaw-ruh-dahn

Elasmosaurus
E-las-moh-saw-ruhs

Fossil hunter

The first ichthyosaur fossil was discovered around 1811 in Lyme Regis, England, by 12-year-old Mary Anning. Mary went on to find more incredible fossils, many of which were world firsts. Though she was not acknowledged for these discoveries during her lifetime, she is now celebrated for her important contribution to science.

Mary Anning

Fast swimmer

Ichthyosaurs were fast swimmers. They could move their tails quickly from side to side like sharks do. Compare this ichthyosaur to its fossil below.

Ichthyosaur
Ick-thee-uh-sor

Fossil Ichthyosaur

DINOSAUR DISASTER!

Dinosaurs, sea reptiles, and pterosaurs were all wiped out by a huge disaster 66 million years ago. No one knows exactly what happened, but some scientists think that an enormous meteorite struck Earth, which would have caused big changes to the atmosphere, killing many animals and plants—and making the dinosaurs become extinct.

Violent volcanoes

Other scientists say that huge volcanic eruptions threw millions of tons of rocks, hot lava, and poisonous ash clouds into the air, killing the dinosaurs.

Climate change

Some scientists believe that the Earth became much colder and this killed the plants, along with the plant-eating dinosaurs. Eventually, the meat eaters died too, when their source of food ran out.

Survivors!

Even though the dinosaurs died out, we know that many smaller animals survived, including birds, insects, crocodiles, lizards, snakes, and mammals, such as the insect-eating *Morganucodon*, which was the size of a mouse. Many of these survivors have developed and evolved into the animals found on Earth today.

Morganucodon
Mor-gan-uh-coh-dohn

GLOSSARY

Camouflage - a pattern on an animal's skin that helps it to blend in with its surroundings.

Carnivore - a creature that only eats other animals, usually herbivores.

Courtship - what an animal does to attract a mate, so that they can make babies together.

Extinct - an animal or plant becomes extinct when all of its kind have died. Once that happens, the species is lost forever and cannot be brought back to life.

Fossil - the impression or remains of a prehistoric plant or animal that have been preserved in rock.

Herbivore - a creature that only eats plants.

Mammal - a warm-blooded animal that gives birth to live young, has a backbone, and has fur or hair.

Predator - an animal that hunts other animals.

Prehistoric - from a long, long time ago, before anything was written down.

Prey - an animal that is hunted by another animal.

Reptile - a cold-blooded creature that lays eggs and has dry, scaly skin.

Rival - a competitor for the same thing.

INDEX